I CAN READ IT ALL BY MYSELF

Beginner Books

This book belongs to ...

_____

©Illus. Dr. Seuss 1957

New Tricks I Can Do!

Robert Lopshire

BEGINNER BOOKS

A Division of Random House, Inc.

http://www.randomhouse.com/

Library of Congress Cataloging-in-Publication Data
Lopshire, Robert.
New tricks I can do! / by Robert Lopshire.
    p.   cm.
SUMMARY: Asked to leave the circus because the audiences have seen all his tricks,
Spot the dog hopes to show them new tricks by turning different colors and
changing the shape of his spots.
ISBN 0-679-87715-0 (trade) — 0-679-97715-5 (lib. bdg.)
[1. Dogs—Fiction. 2. Circus—Fiction. 3. Color—Fiction. 4. Stories in rhyme.]
I. Title.
PZ8.3.L862Ne 1996
[E]—dc20
95-36104

Printed in Melrose Park, Illinois, U.S.A.   SP20001939JAN2022
Early Moments Edition   Item #: 00001-693

Hello there, Spot.

How do you do?

You don't look good...

What's wrong with you?

The circus said
that I must go.
They say most folks
have seen my show.

Folks saw my spots
up in the air.
Folks saw my spots
most everywhere.
The circus says
that's all I do.
The circus wants
somebody new.
But I have more
that I can do...
all kinds of tricks—
and all brand-new!

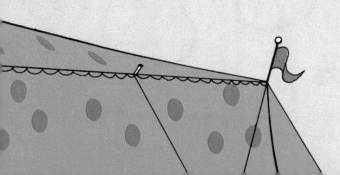

What are these tricks
you say are new?

Please show us some.

Oh yes, please do!

I'll show you both
a trick or two.
Like this one here
where I turn blue.
The circus folks
will say, Please stay,
when they see me
turn blue this way.

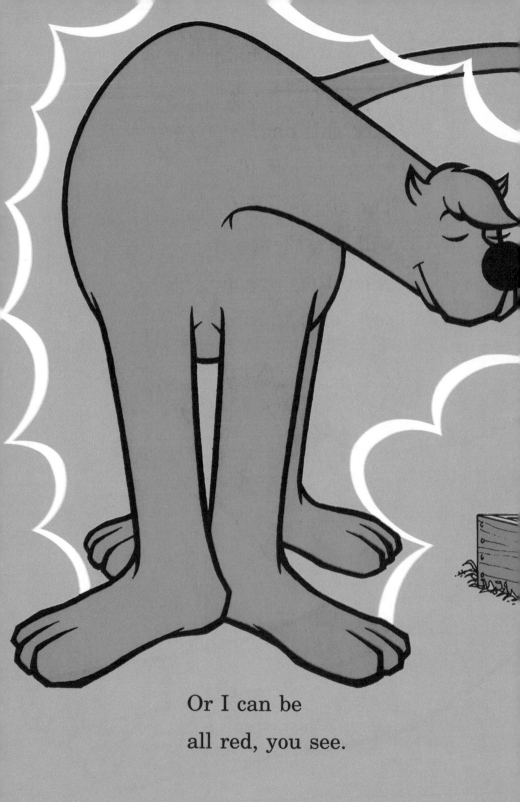

Or I can be
all red, you see.

Or I can be...

...a yellow me!

They'll like these tricks
that I can do.
And I have more
to show to you!

I can be green,

like this, you know...

...or violet
from head to toe.

These things are new
as new can be!
Can you do more?
If so, let's see!

I can make
each spot be square,
in any color
that I care...
Those circus folks
will want me back,
when they see me
in squares of black.

I know that these
would please them too.
And so would...

Stripes!

In pink and blue!

And I have more
that I can do,
so watch me,
watch me now, you two...

As I do this—
and this is new—
I make myself
red, white, and blue!

And there is more,
much more I do,
so watch me now.
Watch, watch, you two!

Like this one here,
you'll like, I know...
when I do this
from top to toe!

Those circus folks
will like this one.
This kind of trick
is never done!

They'd take me back
if they just knew
all of the tricks
that I can do!

They'd take me back,
they'd be so glad,
if they saw me,
like this, in plaid.
The circus says
that I am through,
but I have more
that I can do!

Like this trick here
I've done for you.
It's just one more
that I can do.
Tell me, tell me
now, you two.
How do you like
the tricks I do?

With all the tricks
you've seen today,
will the circus ask
for me to stay?

We like these tricks
that you can do,
but the circus is
all wrong for you!
With tricks this good,
you need to be
where folks can see you...

...on TV!

I CAN READ IT ALL BY MYSELF

Beginner Books